EXCAVATING THE PAST

THE VIKING WORLD

Christine Hatt

Heinemann Library
Chicago, Illinois

Customer Service 888-454-2279
Visit our website at www.heinemannlibrary.com

Designed by Carole Binding
Originated by Ambassador Litho Ltd
Printed in China by WKT Company Limited

09 08 07 06 05
10 9 8 7 6 5 4 3 2 1

Library of Congress Cataloging-in-Publication Data

Hatt, Christine.
  The Viking world / Christine Hatt.
    v. cm. -- (Excavating the past)
Includes bibliographical references and index.
Contents: The Vikings and archeology -- Viking society -- Daily life --
Trade and towns -- War and weapons -- Ships and seafaring -- Art,
learning and religion -- Archeology today.
  ISBN 1-4034-4841-8 (Library binding) -- ISBN 1-4034-5461-2 (pbk.)
  1. Vikings--Juvenile literature. 2. Civilization, Viking--Juvenile
literature. 3. Excavations (Archaeology)--Scandinavia--Juvenile
literature. 4. Scandinavia--Antiquities--Juvenile literature. [1.
Vikings. 2. Excavations (Archaeology)--Scandinavia.] I. Title. II.
Series.
  DL65.H38 2004
  948'.022--dc22
                                              2003023733

Acknowledgments
The author and publisher are grateful to the following for permission to reproduce photographs: pp. 5, 15 top, 20, 23 top, 23 bottom Statens Historiska Museum, Stockholm/Werner Forman Archive; p. 6 Universitetetsbiblioteket, Uppsala, Sweden/Werner Forman Archive; pp. 7, 9 bottom, 10, 11, 28 bottom, 31 bottom Viking Ship Museum, Bygdoy/Werner Forman Archive; p. 9 top O. Vaering/University Museum of Cultural Heritage, University of Oslo, Norway; pp. 12, 17, 28 top, 35 Werner Forman Archive; p. 14 Alamy; pp. 15 bottom, 19, 21, 25, 32 York Archaeological Trust; p. 16 Ove Holst/University Museum of Cultural Heritage, University of Oslo, Norway; pp. 18, 37 Thjodminjasafn, Reykjavik, Iceland (National Museum)/Werner Forman Archive; p. 22 Ted Spiegel/Corbis; p. 26 top BBC Photo Archives; p. 26 bottom Liverpool City Museum, Liverpool, England/Werner Forman Archive; p. 27 Upplsndsmuseet, Uppsala, Sweden/Werner Forman Archive; p. 29 Werner Karrasch/The Viking Ship Museum, Denmark; pp. 30, 34, 35 bottom, 36 top, 36 bottom, 40, 41 The Art Archive; p. 31 top Malcolm Gibb; pp. 38, 42 Topham/Polfoto; p. 39 Carmen Redondo/Corbis; p. 43 Dan Carlsson, Gotland University.

Cover photograph of a Viking house in Jarlshof, Shetland (England), reproduced with permission of Corbis. Small photograph of a Viking nobleman's necklace reproduced with permission of Werner Forman.

The publisher would like to thank Dr. Ailsa Mainman, Assistant Director of the York Archaeological Trust, for her help in the preparation of this book.

Every effort has been made to contact copyright holders of any material reproduced in this book. Any omissions will be rectified in subsequent printings if notice is given to the publisher.

Some words are shown in bold, **like this.** You can find out what they mean by looking in the glossary.

CONTENTS

THE VIKING AGE

The people known as the Vikings came from three countries in northwest Europe—Denmark, Norway, and Sweden. The period known as the Viking Age began when some of them left their homelands in the late 8th century C.E. For about 300 years, Vikings **raided**, explored, and traded with many countries. They also founded many settlements, some of which continued to exist long after the Viking Age was over.

A changing world

In the 700s, most people from Scandinavia (the area of Europe containing Denmark, Norway, and Sweden) were farmers. Then important changes began to affect their way of life. It was probably these changes

▼ *Viking settlements often grew up on coasts and riverbanks, as they were the first places the invaders reached in their powerful ships. Some settlements were also founded on fertile farmland, while others developed from existing towns.*

that led men to sail away in search of wealth and adventure. Scandinavians called this activity going "a-viking," from which the name "Viking" probably comes.

One of the changes was population growth. As the number of people increased, it became more difficult to find good land to farm—so people started to look elsewhere. Another change was increased contact with other parts of Europe, where strong new countries were developing. Sometimes this contact took the form of trade, and important trading towns emerged. Sometimes the Vikings seized opportunities to attack and rob rich settlements and **monasteries**.

A third change was growing violence between men within Scandinavia who were fighting for power. Some men were probably forced out of their homelands by rivals. Some men chose to leave so that they could go raiding and use their **loot** to pay their supporters. Others may have decided that they could not win at home, so would set up new settlements abroad.

Ship-building skills

The Vikings could travel long distances because they were expert ship-builders. As well as narrow wooden **longships** for sailing to war, they built wider ships for taking people and supplies to establish settlements, and strong vessels called *knorrs* for carrying trade goods. All Viking ships had both sails and oars.

▲ ▼ *Archaeologists found these coins depicting Viking longships in the Viking marketplace at Birka, Sweden.*

Expansion and settlement

The first known Viking **raid** took place in 793, when Norwegians attacked a **monastery** on the English island of Lindisfarne. For the next 50 years, Norwegian and Danish Vikings continued to steal goods and terrorize people, not only in England, but also in other European lands. Then, from the mid-800s, their tactics changed and they began to found settlements, eventually reaching North America. Meanwhile Swedish Vikings, known as *Rus,* traveled eastward and soon gave their name to a new land—Russia.

As Vikings traveled the world, major changes continued to take place at home. Gradually, the fighting between rival leaders ended and Scandinavia **converted** from **paganism** to Christianity. By the 11th century in Denmark and Norway, and by the 12th century in Sweden, kings and queens were in control of united countries and daily life had become more stable. The Viking Age was over.

EYEWITNESS

"And they came to the church of Lindisfarne, laid everything waste [destroyed everything] . . ., trampled the holy places with polluted feet, dug up the altars and seized all the treasures . . ."

(An 8th-century account of the Viking raid on Lindisfarne, by Simeon of Durham)

▽ *Snorri Sturluson's book retelling the Viking myths is known as the "Prose Edda."*

WHO WAS Snorri Sturluson?

Snorri Sturluson was a Christian writer in Iceland in the 1200s. He was interested in the Vikings who had settled in his homeland in around 870, so he learned all that he could about them. Later, he wrote books known as **sagas** *about what he had discovered. One book retold* **myths** *about the Viking gods. Another book was a history of the kings of Norway. Experts think that the books are great literature, but do not think that they are always reliable guides to the past because they were written so long after the Viking Age.*

Learning more from archaeology

Historians can discover some facts about the Viking Age by reading documents from the time. However, few documents remain, and they are often unreliable. To learn more, experts turn to archaeology—the study of the past through the examination of **artifacts** and **ruins**. **Archaeologists**, many from Scandinavia, have been **excavating** Viking sites since the 1800s. Many archaeologists were driven by a new pride in Scandinavian history, and a wish to show that there was more to Viking culture than violence.

In the 21st century, excavations are continuing in many places. Although much has already been discovered, there is still more to learn about the daring raiders, traders, and settlers who left their Scandinavian homelands many hundreds of years ago.

▷ *Among the most spectacular Viking discoveries made by archaeologists was a burial site at Oseberg in Norway. This carving of a Viking face is from a beautiful wooden cart found at the site.*

Archaeology Challenge

Archaeologists are always looking for new techniques to help them. For example many are now turning to the science of genetics, the study of how characteristics of living things pass from generation to generation. Genetic information is stored in DNA, a substance in human **cells.** By comparing the DNA of modern humans in the Viking homelands with the DNA of modern humans in places where the Vikings settled, scientists hope to discover which people around the world are descended from Scandinavians.

DID YOU KNOW? The fiercest Viking warriors were called *berserkers*. This is the origin of the word "berserk."

VIKING SOCIETY

Viking society was made up of three groups: kings, queens, and **nobles** at the top; **freemen** in the middle; and slaves at the bottom. Royal people and nobles were usually rich and powerful, while the wealth of freemen depended on how much land they owned. There were several types of slave. Experts think that some Vikings were born into slavery, some became temporary slaves while they were in debt, and others became slaves after they were captured during **raids** overseas.

The Oseberg ship burial

Vikings sometimes buried their dead in ships, then built an earth mound on top. This may have been because they believed that after death people had to travel to a new world. People usually buried possessions that they thought the dead person would need with the body. The quality of these **grave goods** often showed how important a person was in Viking society.

In 1904 **archaeologists**, led by Professor Gabriel Gustafsson, **excavated** a ship burial in Oseberg, Norway. They discovered not only a magnificently carved wooden ship from the 800s, but an exceptional collection of grave goods. The grave goods included a four-wheeled cart, four **sledges**, **tapestries** made of silk and wool. There were also everyday items, such as spades and sewing equipment. Experts think that there had once been fine jewelry in the ship as well, but that it had been stolen by grave-robbers.

Archaeology Challenge

The skeletons at Oseberg were buried in a wooden chamber. Since the chamber was made of oak, archaeologists were able to use a technique called tree-ring dating to find out the age of the wood. The technique works because tree trunks grow a new ring of wood around their centers every year. Each ring varies in width, as each year has different weather conditions. So, by counting the rings, experts can tell how old wood is. At Oseberg, they found that the burial chamber wood had been cut down in 834.

WHO WAS Gabriel Gustafsson?

Gabriel Gustafsson was a Swedish professor, who at the time of the Oseberg excavation was director of the University Museum in Oslo, Norway. He learned about the ship burial mound from a local farmer who brought some pieces of wood from the site to show him. Gustafsson instantly recognized the importance of the find. He never forgot the date in August 1903 when he learned about the ship burial: it was his 50th birthday!

△ Gabriel Gustafsson, the leader of the Oseberg excavations, is in the middle of this picture, with his right arm raised to his waist.

Royal remains?

Archaeologists also discovered two skeletons in the grave. One belonged to a woman about 50 years old, the other to a woman between 20 and 30. As the grave goods were so luxurious, experts believe that one of the women was a queen or noblewoman. They also think that the other woman may have been a slave. In Viking times, slaves were sometimes killed and buried alongside the dead person whom they had served in life.

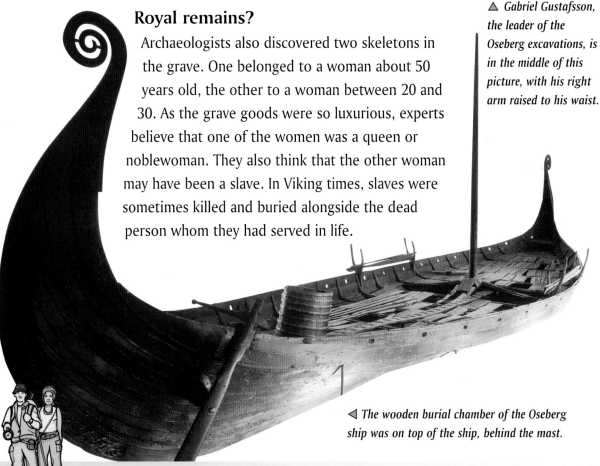

◁ The wooden burial chamber of the Oseberg ship was on top of the ship, behind the mast.

Rich and poor

Information from the grave

Archaeologists are not sure which of the Oseberg skeletons was the queen and which was the slave. But, the fact that grave-robbers had cut off the right hand and left upper arm of the older woman provided a clue. The thieves probably removed these body parts to steal the jewelry on them. So it is likely that the woman was wearing precious rings and bracelets. This suggests, but does not prove, that she was of **noble** birth.

Experts have been able to find out much more about wealthy Vikings by examining the Oseberg **grave goods**. This site and other graves discovered across the Viking world have also taught them a little about slaves.

A cart—and horses

This four-wheeled cart found at Oseberg was probably designed to carry the dead to their home in the afterlife. It was not an everyday vehicle—its sides were covered in elaborate carvings of people, snakes, and other animals. The quality of the carvings suggests that they were made in a royal workshop, and also shows the high rank and wealth of at least one of the grave's inhabitants.

The people who arranged the Oseberg burial did not forget that the cart and its precious cargo would need to be pulled along. Archaeologists found the skeletons of about twelve horses nearby.

◁ *This is some of the detailed carving on the Oseberg cart.*

Beautiful beds

Ordinary Vikings slept on benches or on the floor, so the beds found at Oseberg were further evidence that a rich woman was buried there. One of the five beds **excavated** was in the front part of the ship, outside the burial chamber. Like the ship and cart, it was decorated with animal carvings. The other beds were inside. Two contained the skeletons and had **tapestries** made of silk and wool hung around them—more goods that were too expensive for ordinary Vikings to buy.

▽ *The tapestries from the Oseberg beds were damaged, but it is still possible to pick out the design of a cart being pulled along.*

Women and wealth

The Oseberg burial clearly shows that Viking women were able to enjoy wealth and status. Even ordinary women whose husbands had gone "a-viking" were allowed to run their farms. Women could also own and inherit land, but rarely did so if they had brothers or sons. They even had the right to divorce their husbands and to take half the goods that they had jointly owned.

Silent slaves

Documents such as law codes and traveler accounts show historians that large numbers of slaves worked in Scandinavia during the Viking Age. However, archaeologists have found few **artifacts** that tell them about slave life. It is not possible to tell which graves are those of slaves, and slaves buried with their owners often had no grave goods. The Oseberg slave woman—if she was a slave—is certainly not able to speak clearly to us through the objects in her grave.

How society was governed

In the Viking homelands, society was governed by local **assemblies** called *Things*. Members of *Things* discussed important political matters, made laws, and decided punishments for law-breaking. Every Viking **freeman** was allowed to attend and speak at these gatherings, which usually took place once a year.

The Vikings often set up *Things* in the new places they settled around the world. In fact, these assemblies remained important longer in settlements outside of Scandinavia than inside, where kings gradually took away much of their power.

Discovering Thingvellir

Thingvellir is a natural site in southwest Iceland. It was created thousands of years ago when hot, molten lava poured out of Earth and hardened to form amazing rock shapes. The name Thingvellir means "**parliament** plains." It was here that Viking Icelanders held the *Althing*, their national assembly. It took place for two weeks every June or July between 930 and 1271.

The freemen who took part in this national parliament, the first in Europe, came from thirteen district *Things*. They included the chieftain of each district, who was supposed to speak up for the rights and interests of his own people. Most chieftains could ride to Thingvellir on horseback in a day, but a few from eastern Iceland had to trek for seventeen days across difficult country.

WHO WAS Ari Thorgilsson?

Ari Thorgilsson, also known as Ari the Learned, was an Icelandic historian who lived from 1067 to 1148. His most famous work is "The Book of Icelanders," which he wrote in about 1130. It tells the story of the Vikings in Iceland and provides important information about events that took place at Thingvellir. However, like other written works from the period, Ari's book is not completely reliable. Ari himself said that he based the book's contents on old stories told to him by his foster father, his uncle, and a friend.

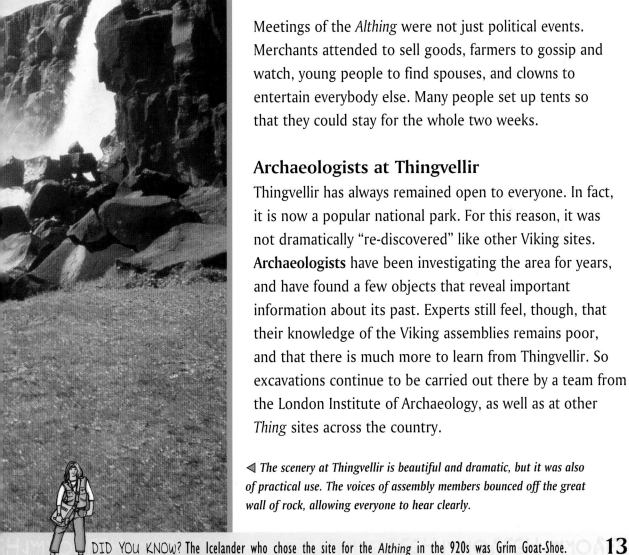

Meetings of the *Althing* were not just political events. Merchants attended to sell goods, farmers to gossip and watch, young people to find spouses, and clowns to entertain everybody else. Many people set up tents so that they could stay for the whole two weeks.

Archaeologists at Thingvellir

Thingvellir has always remained open to everyone. In fact, it is now a popular national park. For this reason, it was not dramatically "re-discovered" like other Viking sites. **Archaeologists** have been investigating the area for years, and have found a few objects that reveal important information about its past. Experts still feel, though, that their knowledge of the Viking assemblies remains poor, and that there is much more to learn from Thingvellir. So excavations continue to be carried out there by a team from the London Institute of Archaeology, as well as at other *Thing* sites across the country.

◁ *The scenery at Thingvellir is beautiful and dramatic, but it was also of practical use. The voices of assembly members bounced off the great wall of rock, allowing everyone to hear clearly.*

Law, crime, and punishment

Excavations at the Thingvellir site, together with research in books and documents, have already revealed important facts about how the Vikings governed themselves. In particular, they have shown how chieftains and ordinary **freemen** at the *Althing* and other **assemblies** made laws, punished crimes, and reached major decisions.

The Law-Speaker and the Law Rock

A small group of people at the *Althing* was responsible for making Iceland's laws. It contained the 13 chieftains and 26 legal experts, two to advise each of the local leaders. The group was led by an official known as the Law-Speaker, who was elected every three years. It was his job to memorize all national laws, and to recite them aloud whenever the **parliament** met. To carry out this demanding task the Law-Speaker stood in a special place at Thingvellir—on top of a huge piece of solidified lava known as the Law Rock.

Crimes and courts

In Viking society, there were frequent disputes between rival chieftains or other leaders. This often led to violence, and even murder. Men who had committed such crimes were usually judged by members of a *Thing*, and could be sent away from their homeland forever as a punishment. As judgements, like laws, were rarely written down, legal experts tried to memorize them exactly.

Iceland also had five courts to consider serious crimes. Four courts had juries to decide whether a person was innocent or guilty. Judges in a special, fifth court ruled on very difficult cases. These cases often involved age-old, bitter clashes between the mightiest Viking chieftains and their families. Many of the **sagas** describe such complex legal battles.

Religion

Members of *Things* did not concern themselves only with crime. The most famous decision made at the *Althing*, for example, was about religion. By the 900s, some Icelanders had become Christians, but others still worshiped pagan gods. In 1000, members of the *Althing* debated the subject and the Law-Speaker announced that everyone should adopt Christianity.

Bishops and crosiers

Gradually, Christianity replaced **paganism** in all the Scandinavian countries. As more people became Christians, churches were built and **bishops** were appointed. The first bishop in Iceland was Isleif Gissurarson, who was appointed in 1056. Then as now, bishops carried long sticks, called **crosiers,** with a cross or hook at the top. The crosier shown on the left was found at Birka, Sweden.

EYEWITNESS

"'It seems to me good sense,' he said, 'that . . . we all have one law and custom; . . . if we divide the law, we will divide the peace.' Then Thorgeir [the Law-Speaker] declared the law, that all . . . people in the land should become Christian. . ."

(From "The Book of the Icelanders" by Ari Thorgilsson)

Assemblies around the world

There were *Things* all over the Viking world and modern place-names often provide a clue as to where they were. For example, Tingwall in the Orkney Islands and Tynwald on the Isle of Man (right) were both once sites of these Viking assemblies.

The daily life of most Vikings involved a great deal of hard work. Men farmed their land and hunted to provide food for their families. Women looked after their children and houses, and cooked meals using the food that the men brought home.

Most ordinary Viking men were farmers. They kept cows, sheep, pigs, goats, and chickens, and grew cereal crops, such as rye and barley, as well as many vegetables. A farmer's day began at sunrise and lasted until darkness fell again. Men went hunting and fishing, both to find extra food and for sport.

Viking women were based at home. Houses were rectangular and usually made of wood. Around the walls of the main room were benches to sit or sleep on, and in the center was a **hearth** used for cooking and heating. Some houses had a separate area in which cows were kept, and it was a woman's job to milk them. Women also cared for the sick by using herbs and magic charms.

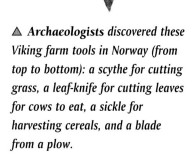

△ *Archaeologists discovered these Viking farm tools in Norway (from top to bottom): a scythe for cutting grass, a leaf-knife for cutting leaves for cows to eat, a sickle for harvesting cereals, and a blade from a plow.*

Discovering Brattahlid

The Vikings often built farms where they settled overseas. In the late 900s, Vikings led by Erik the Red arrived in Greenland from Iceland. They made their homes in two main areas: the Eastern Settlement, where Erik built a farm named Brattahlid, and the Western Settlement, about 404 miles (650 kilometers) further north.

▷ *At Brattahlid, in Greenland, the Vikings built their settlement close to the coast where they landed. The icebergs in the background are evidence of the cold climate.*

As the years passed, more and more Vikings came to Greenland, until there were many hundreds of farms. The farm buildings were usually not made from wood, as in Scandinavia, because Greenland has few trees. Instead, people generally built their homes from stones and **turf**. Experts believe that Viking settlement in Greenland came to an end during the 1300s.

Excavations at Brattahlid and other Greenland sites have helped archaeologists learn much more about daily life in Viking times. The first excavations at Brattahlid were carried out in 1932 by archaeologists from the National Museum of Denmark. They investigated a cluster of **ruins** that they believed might have been Erik the Red's farm. In 1961, Danish archaeologists began further work near this original site, after builders accidentally unearthed a Viking cemetery.

WHO WAS Erik the Red?

Erik the Red was a 10th-century Norwegian with a fiery temper. He had to leave his own country after a Thing found him guilty of murder. He settled in Iceland, where he married and began a farm. But after more murders, he was sent away from that country, too. So, he left to found the Greenland colony. Erik is also the father of Leif Eriksson, the Viking who in about 1000 founded a colony in North America.

Food and farming

A central hall

The cluster of buildings at Brattahlid that were **excavated** in 1932 had a rectangular stone and **turf** hall in the middle. The walls of the hall were thick, to protect the people inside from Greenland's icy weather. Under the floor was a man-made channel through which water flowed into the house, and at the center was a large **hearth** for cooking. Experts think that people in Brattahlid gathered in the hall to eat their evening meal.

Two meals a day

Vikings usually ate two meals a day: bread and porridge in the morning, and a heavy, meat-based dinner in the evening with large amounts of beer. In Scandinavia, the meat came from farm animals, such as cows, and wild animals, such as reindeer. The many animal bones that were discovered in Greenland showed **archaeologists** that Vikings there adapted to local conditions by hunting and eating seals and caribou, a type of large deer.

Fantasy or Fact?

Experts are certain that Erik the Red lived at Brattahlid. But archaeology has shown that the hall and other **ruins** excavated in 1932 could not have belonged to him because they date from the 1200s and 1300s. Older remains underneath the hall may have been his farm. Excavations at the Viking cemetery in the 1960s and 1970s led to the discovery of another group of buildings that may have been Erik's original home.

Relaxation

Having gathered in the Brattahlid hall for their evening meal, people would have listened to music, poems, and stories from **sagas.** They would have also enjoyed board games, including a Viking favorite called *hnefatafl.* The game probably involved two players fighting "wars" on a board. This is a playing piece from a *hnefatafl* game set.

Farm buildings

In Scandinavia, Viking farmers shared their homes with animals. This was true in Brattahlid, too. At one end of the hall was a byre—a shelter for cows. Rooms for storing crops were also attached to the building, and there were four barns and two more byres nearby. Byres contain partitions that keep cows apart. In Brattahlid, these were made of stone or whale shoulder bones, as wood was scarce in Greenland.

△ *Sometimes archaeologists produce reconstructions to show how people lived in the past. Here, the knowledge archaeologists have gained from Viking remains and* **artifacts** *has been used to re-create a life-size model of a loom. The circular loom weights can be seen at the bottom of the threads.*

Cloth and clothes

In one Brattahlid barn, archaeologists found a small, broken circular object with a hole in the middle. This was a stone **loom** weight. Viking weavers hung weights on the end of the vertical threads in the cloth they were making. In this way, the weights stopped the material from becoming loose. Every Viking home contained a loom on which women made fabric to turn into clothes.

People's clothes depended on how important they were. Most males wore shirts, short tunics, and **breeches.** The clothes of rich men were made from linen and fine wool, while the clothes of poor men were roughly woven, ill-fitting garments of coarse wool cloth. Females usually wore full-length, long-sleeved tunics with long aprons over the top, but the clothing of rich women was of better quality. Clothing was fastened with dress pins or brooches made of bone, silver, or bronze, depending on what could be afforded.

M ost Vikings were farmers, but many were traders who earned money by buying and selling. When not traveling abroad, these men usually spent their time in towns. There they met other merchants and bought trade goods from local craftspeople.

The Vikings were able to establish trade networks because they were expert sailors and built sturdy ships. The ships allowed them to carry cargoes across the seas and along great European rivers, such as the Dneiper and Volga. The Vikings also succeeded because their homelands produced many desirable goods to sell, including furs, hunting falcons, **amber**, walrus **ivory**, and iron. The Vikings traded in people, too, supplying slaves to eastern lands.

Viking traders bought as well as sold. Among the many goods they imported from Western Europe, Russia, the Middle East, and Asia were silver, spices, wine, and silks.

▲ *These coins from the Middle East and the Byzantine Empire were found in Viking burial sites in Sweden. They prove to* **archaeologists** *that Viking traders had traveled far from Scandinavia.*

Discovering Birka

The Swedes were perhaps the greatest Viking traders. From their homelands they sailed east to Russia, the Arab World, and the Byzantine Empire (in the area of modern Turkey). They established trading links with these regions, and with places even further away, such as China.

WHO WAS Hjalmar Stolpe?

Hjalmar Stolpe trained not as an archaeologist, but as an entomologist (insect expert). When he went to Birka in 1871, his aim was to find prehistoric flies trapped in pieces of amber, but he soon realized that the town was a major Viking site. As well as excavating graves, Stolpe examined part of the "Black Earth" area. Unlike many archaeologists of the time, who were little more than treasure-hunters, Stolpe worked as scientifically as he could.

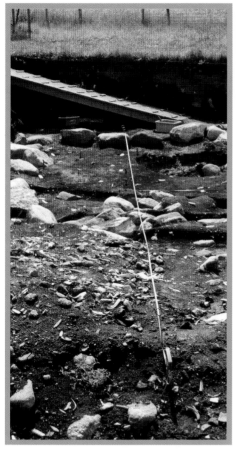

△ *The remains of food, buildings, and more have darkened the soil in the part of Birka where most people lived. Therefore the area is known as the "Black Earth" area.*

As business increased, special trading towns developed back in Sweden. One such town was Birka, which was founded in about 800 on an island named Björkö, at the edge of the Baltic Sea. Birka was home to foreign merchants and to native Swedes, both traders and craftspeople. Experts believe that no more than about 900 people ever lived there, but it would have been a busy, noisy place, full of men and women from many lands.

The importance of Birka was discovered due to the work of one determined Swedish archaeologist, Hjalmar Stolpe. Starting in 1871, he **excavated** more than 1,100 graves outside the town's walls. He found many precious **grave goods**, including silver from the Middle East and silks from the Byzantine Empire.

There have been several more major excavations at Birka since Stolpe's time. From the late 1960s to the mid-1990s, archaeological teams, led by Dr. Björn Ambrosiani of Sweden's Museum of National Antiquities, have explored the "Black Earth" area of Birka where most people lived.

DID YOU KNOW? The furs Vikings sold came from animals such as martens, squirrels, and beavers. **21**

Town life

The 1990s excavations in Birka's "Black Earth" area provided much information about daily life in this important Swedish trading town. The excavations also enabled experts to take a close-up look at workshops where men did metalwork, a craft at which the Vikings excelled.

Homes by the harbor

Some of Sweden's trading centers emerged naturally, but Birka was a planned settlement, with houses and workshops enclosed inside a defensive wall and protected by a fort. The streets linking houses were very narrow, and many led down to small **jetties** that extended out into the harbor. When trading ships arrived, they moored next to the jetties so that people could walk out to unload or examine goods.

Archaeology Challenge

Both during and since Viking times, the sea level around Birka has risen and fallen quite dramatically. This fact often makes it hard for **archaeologists** to work out exactly where to **excavate.** In the late 1960s, Dr. Björn Ambrosiani was trying to find the Viking town harbor. He knew that in the 800s, the sea had covered more of the island where Birka stands than it does now. So, instead of digging around the modern shoreline, he dug inland. He found a jetty on the first day of excavations!

▽ *At this reconstructed Viking village, the houses have wattle-and-daub walls and turf roofs.*

Viking houses

At Birka and in other parts of Scandinavia, house frames were made of sturdy wooden posts. The posts were joined together with either woven twigs, called wattle, or planks. If wattle was used, it was coated with daub, a sticky mixture of clay, dung, and water that dried to make it waterproof. This type of construction is known as wattle-and-daub. Roofs were made of wood, thatch, or **turf.**

Craft workshops

Many of Sweden's trading towns and other centers contained craft workshops. Some produced jewelry and other goods for merchants to sell abroad. But many craft items from Birka were probably given to local farmers in exchange for food, as little could be produced in the town itself.

The 1990s excavations at Birka revealed much more about the town's workshops, where a wide variety of metal objects were made. Workshop rooms were small, with wattle-and-daub walls and **hearths** around the sides. It was important to keep the hearth fires burning, as they were used for melting metal. Experts think that screens were probably placed in front of the hearths to stop drafts.

From clay to bronze

Viking metalworkers made tools and weapons from iron, and jewelry from gold, silver, and bronze. Objects, such as this bronze brooch, were made by first creating clay molds (below). While the clay was soft, an object that already had the required shape was pressed into it, to transfer the pattern. After the molds had dried hard, hot bronze was poured inside. The bronze then cooled and hardened, so that by the time the mold was opened it had taken on the pattern in the clay. Archaeologists at Birka found many pieces of broken clay molds. From them, they worked out that the local craftspeople made not only elaborate bronze brooches, but also pendants, keys, belts, and more. The metal used was often recycled. Old items were melted down and re-used. Excavations also uncovered metalworking tools.

Vikings were expert and eager warriors. Rival chieftains and their followers fought each other at home and abroad. Hit-and-run **raiders** attacked coastal **monasteries** and villages across northwest Europe. And mighty armies, seeking conquest as well as treasure, waged long and brutal wars against foreign enemies.

▲ *In 878 the Anglo-Saxons pushed the Vikings out of Wessex and part of Mercia. The areas north and east of the red line were controlled by the Vikings and became known as the* Danelaw.

When Vikings arrived in Greenland they faced no opposition, as no one else lived there. However, when they decided to settle in England, the Vikings first had to conquer its **Anglo-Saxon** inhabitants. Viking **campaigns** against the English began in 866, when a powerful group of fighting men, who became known as the Great Army, arrived from Denmark. By 874 the Vikings controlled all of England except for the kingdom of Wessex. In 878 the people of Wessex, led by King Alfred the Great, defeated the Vikings at the Battle of Edington, forcing them to return to north and east England. These Viking-ruled territories became known as the *Danelaw.*

Discovering Repton

In summer, the Great Army moved around England from battle to battle. Then, as the weather became cold and unsuitable for fighting, they built camps for the winter. In 1974, **archaeologists** discovered by chance the remains of a Viking winter camp at Repton in Derbyshire.

▷ *Archaeologists find many Viking **artifacts** in areas of England that were part of the Danelaw. These combs were found in York (Viking name: Jorvik), which was captured by the Great Army in 867.*

Repton was also the site of an Anglo-Saxon church and monastery, where monks once lived. It was this site that archaeologists Berthe and Martin Biddle were **excavating** when they discovered the remains of an earth bank with a ditch alongside. The bank and ditch swept in a semi-circle down to the Trent River, which joined the two ends of the curve to create a "D" shape. The archaeologists knew that the Danes built **enclosures** in this shape for protection.

Trent River

Bank

Ditch

Anglo-Saxon church

Mass burial

Anglo-Saxon chapel

D-shaped enclosure

+Burial site

△ *Remains of a bank and ditch at Repton were evidence that Vikings had set up camp there.*

Excavations at Repton continued until 1988 and confirmed that the Great Army had almost certainly spent the winter of 873–874 there. The excavations also showed that the **pagan** Viking soldiers had seized the church from its Christian inhabitants and built the defensive earth bank around it.

WHO WAS Rollo?

Like England, France was a target of campaigns by Viking armies. The most famous of these Viking armies was led by a Norwegian known as Rollo. In 911 the ruler of France, Charles the Simple, tried to persuade Rollo to stop his attacks by giving him land in northern France. Rollo took the land, but continued fighting. Many Vikings settled on Rollo's land and adopted the French language and way of life. They became known as Normans, and their land known as Normandy. These were the Normans who invaded and conquered England in 1066.

Warriors and weapons

Hundreds of skeletons were found at the Repton site. The most revealing skeleton belonged to a warrior who had died in battle. However, it was hard to discover who many of the others were or what had killed them.

Death of a fighting man

Viking graves were scattered around the church at Repton, including one belonging to a man about 40 years old. Examination of his bones showed that a savage blow to the hip had caused his death.

There were many items in the grave with the skeleton. A silver pendant shaped like a hammer was hanging around the neck of the skeleton. The hammer was the symbol of Thor, the Viking god of thunder, who was believed to fight giants and demons. Weapons in the grave, including a sword, scabbard (sword-holder), and a selection of knives, made it clear the man was a warrior.

Weapons and armor

Every Viking **freeman** had the right to own weapons, but the quality and type of weapon depended on a man's status. Professional soldiers and rich men always had at least one long, sometimes decorated, sword with a double-cutting edge of sharp steel. They also carried knives that could kill an enemy at close range, and spears that could be thrust into an enemy from a distance. Some also had simple, metal-bladed battleaxes, but these were more often the weapons of ordinary working men who did not fight often.

Armor

In battle, many high-ranking men wore padded jackets under tunics made of chain mail (linked metal rings). They also had large, round, wooden shields and pointed iron helmets with protective metal bands covering the nose and cheeks. The front of this helmet, found in a boat grave in Sweden, is protected by chain mail. Ordinary fighting men had helmets and shields but little else.

Mass burial mystery

In 1986, **archaeologists excavated** the site of a former **Anglo-Saxon** chapel just outside Repton's D-shaped bank. There they found a mass grave with the remains of 249 people that the Vikings had buried inside it. One man had been buried on his own in the middle, suggesting that he was a chieftain, but unfortunately his skeleton had already been removed.

Coins discovered in the grave suggest that it was dug when the Great Army was in Repton, but the bones showed that the men had not died in battle. About one-fifth of the skeletons belonged to women, perhaps Anglo-Saxon wives of Viking men, and they had not died in fighting either. Experts' best guess is that disease swept through the camp and surrounding areas in the winter of 873–874, killing many of the people. But the identity of the missing chieftain remains a mystery.

Fantasy or Fact?

The warrior's grave by the church in Repton contained a small bag with a bird bone and a boar tusk inside. The animal remains may have had some practical use, but experts believe that they were probably magic charms designed to keep away evil.

SHIPS AND SEAFARING

Without their superb ships, the Vikings could not have made the impact on the world that they did, either as warriors or as traders. The Vikings showed that they valued their sea-going craft by burying important people in ships, for example at Oseberg, and by sometimes arranging stones on graves in boat shapes. They also carved pictures of ships, for example at Gotland.

△ *These stone grave markers in Lindholm Høje, Denmark, are arranged in boat shapes.*

Archaeologists began to discover the remains of Viking ships in the 1800s. In 1880, a ship 75 feet (23 meters) long was unearthed from a burial mound in Gokstad, Norway. It had been built in about 850, possibly as a royal barge, and then became the grave of a king. The craft was built from oak planks and had holes in the sides to hold sixteen pairs of oars. Its sail was made of red and white fabric strips that could be hung downward or interwoven to make a check pattern.

Three smaller boats were also found in the burial mound, telling archaeologists more about everyday Viking ships, such as fishing boats. More information was revealed by the Oseberg burial in 1904. However, it was many years later before experts had the chance to examine a far greater variety of Viking vessels at a single site, Roskilde **Fjord** in Denmark.

△ *This ship was discovered in a burial mound in Gokstad, Norway.*

Discovering Roskilde

In the 11th century, Denmark and Norway were at war. To keep the Norwegians out of Roskilde —then Denmark's capital—the Danes blocked the fjord that led up to it by deliberately sinking five ships. The fjord area where the ships went down was named Skuldelev.

About 900 years later, in 1956, divers found a strangely shaped piece of oak in Skuldelev's shallow waters. It proved to be the mast of a Viking ship and led Danish archaeologist and ship expert Dr. Ole Crumlin-Pedersen to begin underwater excavations.

The archaeological team eventually found all five of the ships that had been sunk, and lifted them slowly and gently from the seabed. After so many years underwater, the craft were damaged and had soft, soggy timbers. Even so, it was clear that this was a major find. The experts had discovered two types of warship, a ferry, and two merchant ships for carrying cargo. They were able to rebuild four of the craft, but one warship was too damaged to reconstruct.

△ *The cofferdam around the excavation site at Roskilde was built in 1962, six years after the first discovery there.*

DID YOU KNOW? A replica of the Gokstad ship sailed from Norway to the United States in 1893.

Shipbuilding and navigation

Examination of the ships found at Roskilde and other sites helped **archaeologists** understand more about Viking vessels and how they were built. Other discoveries led them to think more closely about how Vikings found their way across the oceans to distant lands.

Warships

One of the Roskilde warships was too light to be a true Viking **longship,** but the other, the vessel that could not be rebuilt, was exactly the type that struck fear into people's hearts as they saw it approach. In its original state, this ship measured 100 feet (30 meters) from prow (front) to stern (back). It was powered by the wind in its single sail and by 36 oarsmen, 18 on each side. They would have hung their colorful shields over the side of the ship as they rowed.

Merchant ships

The two merchant ships found at Roskilde were wider and shorter than the warships. One was a *knorr,* designed to carry heavy cargoes across open oceans. The other (right) was a lighter type, for use in shallow coastal waters and rivers.

Shipbuilding: special features of Viking ships

All Viking ships were clinker-built, that is, made of slightly overlapping wooden planks. Rivets (metal pins) held the planks together. Oak and pine were commonly used woods. The **hulls** of the ships were not very deep. This made it possible for Viking warriors to sail up to a beach, rather than anchoring out to sea like other vessels. The tactic terrified people under attack on land, who did not realize how close the longships could get until it was too late.

Another important feature of Viking ships was the giant rudders attached underwater at the back. By turning a handle attached to these blades, warriors could steer the ships accurately.

▽ *The prow of a Viking longship was often topped with an elaborate carving in the shape of a dragon's head. The carving was taken down when the ship was at sea.*

◁ *In 1984, the Saga Siglar, a replica of one of the Roskilde ships, sailed around the world. On the voyage, the sailors tested the "Sun compass."*

Navigation skills

Viking sailors learned how to use the positions of the Sun and stars and the direction of the wind to judge where they were and where they were going. They were also skilled at estimating how far and how fast they had traveled. Some people have suggested that the Vikings also had simple tools for **navigation.** In Greenland during the 1940s, an archaeologist found half of what had been a circular wooden object. It had a hole in the middle and notches around the edge. When Danish sailor Captain C. V. Sølver saw it, he suggested it was a form of compass that used the angle of the Sun's rays to show a ship's direction. Trials of this "Sun compass" showed that it worked, but many experts believe that the Vikings never used it.

DID YOU KNOW? The Vikings sometimes named their ships "surf dragon" and "horses of the waves." **31**

Vikings around the world

The Vikings traveled far and wide. There is archaeological evidence that confirms the Vikings reached Russia in the east. But experts were unsure about tales in the **sagas** stating that the Vikings reached North America in the west. Different sagas tell different stories about the Vikings in North America, but experts have tried to work out from them what really happened. They think that the first Viking to see the coast of North America was Bjarni Herjolfsson, who ended up there by mistake while trying to reach Greenland. Later, Leif Eriksson set out to find the land Bjarni had sailed past. He did so in about 1000, and named the region "Vinland" ("Wineland")—perhaps because he saw grapes there. Some experts now think the "grapes" were probably a type of berry.

▷ *The houses at L'Anse-aux-Meadows were made from driftwood covered with turf.*

Fantasy or Fact?

In 1965 Yale University in New Haven, Connecticut, published a map. The map was believed to show Vinland and to date from the mid-1400s. Since it was thought to be based on a Viking map, it seemed to prove that the Vikings had been to North America. Many Viking Age experts were impressed by the document. However, scientific tests in the 1970s showed that the map was a fake. The ink used to create it was first made in the 20th century.

Leif Eriksson and his companions built turf shelters in Vinland, but stayed only for the winter. A few years later, an Icelander named Thorfinn Karlsefni tried to create a permanent farming settlement there. However, bad relations with Native Americans, and the difficulty of obtaining supplies from their homelands, led the Vikings to leave after about three years.

Discovering L'Anse-aux-Meadows

The sagas did not say where in North America Eriksson had landed. The northeast coast seemed a likely place, but grapes have never grown in this cold region. Sadly, there seemed to be no Viking sites to help solve this puzzle. Then, in 1960, Norwegian explorer Helge Ingstad heard about possible Viking remains in L'Anse-aux-Meadows, Newfoundland, an island off the east coast of Canada. He and his wife, **archaeologist** Anne Stine Ingstad, set out to investigate.

Working from 1961 to 1968, the Ingstads found a cluster of eight turf and driftwood houses with the remains of **hearths** and benches inside, in the exact style of Viking homes. They also found Viking-style objects, including a bronze pin and a **spindle** part. Icelandic archaeologists working with the Ingstads **excavated** a **forge** on the site and found a **kiln**, rivets, and other evidence of metalworking. The Ingstads were now convinced that they had found the only known Viking site in North America. In the 1970s a Swedish team of archaeologists confirmed the Ingstads' view. However, whether this cold, grape-free area is the Vinland of the Viking sagas may remain a mystery forever.

Archaeology Challenge

Living things like plants and animals absorb a **radioactive** type of the chemical carbon—called Carbon-14—from the air. When plants and animals die, Carbon-14 decays at a rate that experts know and can measure. As a result, the age of bone, wood, or anything else that was once part of a living thing, can be found by analyzing how much Carbon-14 it contains. Experts used this technique, called radiocarbon dating, to work out the age of the L'Anse-aux-Meadows site. They found that it dated from Viking times.

ART, LEARNING, AND RELIGION

The Vikings were practical people who liked to sail, farm, and trade. They also had cultural and spiritual interests, creating beautiful objects, writing powerful literature, and practicing their faith, whether **paganism** or Christianity. Finds from many sites demonstrate these interests in art, learning, and religion.

Discovering Gotland

Gotland is an island in the Baltic Sea off the coast of Sweden. In Viking times, as now, its rich land was covered in farms. In addition, Gotland was a center of trade because it can be reached easily from other Baltic islands, the Scandinavian mainland, Poland, and Russia.

Evidence of the island's trading links comes from the many coins and other treasures found there. In 1999, for example, two **hoards** were discovered in a single field. They contained 154 pounds (70 kilograms) of silver items, including jewelry and Arab coins.

Gotland is important to **archaeologists** for another reason, too. Its people had a thriving cultural life that, although clearly Viking, was unlike anything else in Scandinavia.

Fantasy or Fact?

*Archaeologists and others have found hundreds of treasure hoards on Gotland, but they are not sure why. Some think that the islanders were pirates who stole these precious goods from ships. Others believe that the islanders were frightened of pirates, so hid valuable belongings underground. A third theory is that the islanders buried their possessions for religious reasons. They may have been saving them for the afterlife or **sacrificing** them to the gods.*

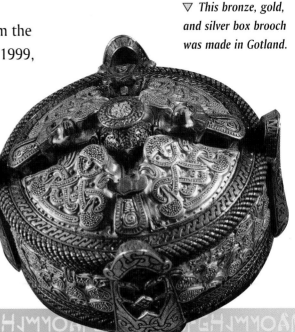

▽ *This bronze, gold, and silver box brooch was made in Gotland.*

▷ These iron-working and carpentry tools were found in a bog at Mästermyr on Gotland.

In addition, they produced huge numbers of goods. There are more pre-Viking and Viking objects on Gotland, an island of 1,158 square miles (3,000 square kilometers), than there are in Sweden itself, which is about 150 times as large!

Marvelous metalwork

Gotland's metalwork has attracted special interest. Even practical items, such as metal fittings on horse harnesses, were decorated with intertwined animals and birds. The island's jewelry was more striking still. The unique, circular box brooches, for example, were covered in beautiful filigree—strands of gold or other metal twisted into intricate shapes.

The swirling animals on Gotland metalwork were copied on the wooden prow of the Oseberg ship, but in a different style. Later, the Oseberg animals were copied, again in a slightly different way. This process continued throughout the Viking Age, so by looking at the style of a piece of metalwork or other art, experts can tell when it was produced.

Picture stones

Despite the beauty of its metalwork, Gotland is famous above all for something else unique—its picture stones. Experts have found about 370 of these carved blocks from the Viking Age and earlier. They were designed as memorials, and are covered in pictures of people, ships, and scenes from **myths**.

▷ The Gotland picture stones are a wonderful source of information about Viking times.

Gods and goddesses

The Viking **pagan** religion included many gods and goddesses, but it is hard to work out exactly what people believed or how they worshiped. For help, experts turn to sources such as the Gotland picture stones and writings called *Eddas.*

There are two *Eddas,* both compiled in Iceland during the 1200s. The *Poetic Edda* contains 39 poems from many periods and several countries. Ten are about the gods of Viking religion.

The *Prose Edda* was put together by Snorri Sturluson. It was designed to help young writers compose new poetry and understand the references to gods and goddesses in existing poetry. Since it contains retellings of all the Viking **myths**, it is very useful to people who want to understand Viking religion.

Picture stories

The Gotland picture stones were carved from the 400s until the end of the Viking Age. It is possible to follow the development of Scandinavian religion through their pictures. The pre-Viking stones often feature a wheel (above). Some experts believe this represents the Sun—evidence that the islanders long ago worshiped this star. The later stones carved by Vikings show many of their pagan gods, including the mighty trio of Odin, Thor, and Freyr. Also portrayed is Valhalla, the great hall thought to be the resting place of Viking warriors who died in battle. The last stones come from the time when Christianity was replacing paganism. Many of them are marked with a cross.

▼ *This scene from a picture stone tells a story from the* **Prose Edda** *about a blacksmith. The hammers and tongs that he used for his work can be seen near the top right of the image.*

The Final Day

Viking mythology did not promise a happy end for the gods. It foretold that they would all die on the Final Day, called Ragnarök, and that the whole world would be destroyed by fire.

Fantasy or Fact?

Little is known about the places where the Vikings worshiped their gods. However, an 11th-century German Christian, named Adam of Bremen, did write a description of a temple that he saw in Uppsala, Sweden. According to him, there were statues of Odin, Thor, and Freyr inside the temple, and both animals and men were **sacrificed** *to them. As a Christian, Adam would probably have been eager to criticize pagan rituals. But modern experts think that sacrifice really was a part of Viking religious practice.*

The Viking gods

The stories of the Viking gods originally came from Germany and other parts of central Europe. There were many versions, but the most powerful and widely worshiped gods appear in them all.

The Viking gods were said to live in a place called Asgard. Odin was the chief god. He performed powerful magic. He also helped warriors and welcomed them to Valhalla, his home, after death. Odin rode an eight-legged horse named Sleipnir.

The figure on the left is Thor, another powerful Viking god. Thor was the god of thunder and lightning. He carried a hammer to defend Asgard and ruled over the sky, often causing storms.

Freyr and his sister Freyia were **fertility** gods. They were responsible for ensuring that people had many children and that the land produced plentiful crops. Some farmers even named their fields after Freyr, in the hope that this would ensure a good harvest.

The arrival of Christianity

The **pagan** beliefs of the Vikings remained strong throughout the 800s. But gradually contact with countries outside their Scandinavian homelands, and the arrival of **missionaries** in Scandinavia, led to the spread of a very different faith—Christianity. The first major missionary to the Vikings was Ansgar, a monk from Germany. He traveled to Denmark and Sweden in the mid-800s, and founded churches in places such as Birka. However, people did not immediately **convert** to Christianity in large numbers.

More than 100 years later, in about 960, King Harald Bluetooth introduced the new religion in Denmark. Then, in the early 11th century, King Olaf Haraldsson forced Norway to accept it. By that time, Norwegian missionaries had already taken Christianity to Iceland, where the *Althing* adopted it in 1000. Leif Eriksson carried the faith to Greenland a short while later. In Sweden, pagan resistance was strong, and so Christianity did not become widespread there until the late 11th century.

EYEWITNESS

"King Olaf laid such stress on all men in his kingdom being Christians that he offered them the choice: be killed, leave the country, or take baptism."

(An account from a saga explaining how Olaf Haraldsson persuaded Norwegian pagans to convert to Christianity)

▷ *These are the* **ruins** *of Gardar Cathedral in Greenland. When still standing, it was more than 98 feet (30 meters) long. Gardar was one of the earliest major Christian sites in the Viking world.*

Discovering Jelling

Jelling was once the home of the kings of Denmark, and is a key site in the story of Christianity's arrival in that country. **Archaeologists** revealed this story by **excavating** two burial mounds, as well as a church and two **rune** stones that stand between them. The tale concerns the Danish King Gorm, who in the 930s refused to accept Christianity, his wife Thyri, and his son Harald Bluetooth.

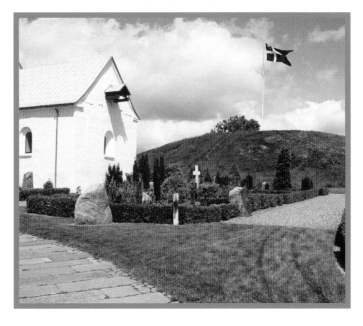

▽ *Rune stones are stones with Viking letters (runes) on them. The rune stones at Jelling stand just outside the church.*

It was widely believed that the North Mound at Jelling contained the body of Queen Thyri. When excavations began there in 1820, experts hoped to confirm this. However, although the mound contained a 10th-century burial chamber, there were no human remains. There were just animal bones and **grave goods**. Excavations of the South Mound, Gorm's supposed burial place, in the 1860s and 1940s, were even less helpful—they found nothing at all.

Archaeologists' luck began to improve in the mid-1960s, when Dr. Knud Krogh from the National Museum of Denmark began to excavate the church. He showed that over time, there had been three separate churches on the site, and he found a grave under the floor of the oldest. The grave dated from the mid-900s, when Harald Bluetooth was on the throne, and contained the skeleton of a man, some jewelry, and some golden threads.

Archaeologists now had the evidence to help them tell the story, but they also had other important evidence. It came from the rune stones.

Runes and writing

Runes are the letters of the Viking alphabet, and Vikings used them to carve messages on stone, wood, bone, and metal. **Archaeologists** use the runic writings to help them solve puzzles of the past, like the story of Jelling.

The Jelling story

From studying the rune stones, experts now believe that the **pagan** King Gorm was buried in the North Mound, but that his bones were removed by his son, Harald Bluetooth. As the larger rune stone states, the Danes **converted** to Christianity during Harald's reign. As a Christian, Harald would have wanted to rebury his father in the church. This means that the bones found there are likely to be Gorm's.

Experts still do not know where Thyri is buried. As the smaller rune stone is a memorial to her, it seems likely that her grave is nearby, possibly in the South Mound.

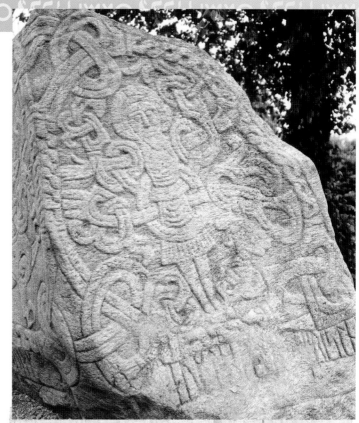

The Jelling stones

The larger rune stone at Jelling has three sides, all of them carved with intertwining, Viking-style designs. One side also carries a picture of Jesus on the cross (above). The runic message is long, but its main words are: "King Harald had this memorial made for Gorm his father and Thyri his mother. It was this Harald who . . . made the Danes Christians." The other rune stone is much smaller, and the writing on it declares: "King Gorm made this memorial to his wife Thyri, Denmark's glory."

The runic alphabet

Runes were used across the Viking world, but were especially common in Sweden. By the Viking Age, there were two runic alphabets, with sixteen symbols in each. The short-twig alphabet was the main form of runes in Norway and Sweden.. The long-branch alphabet was the main form of runes in Denmark, but sometimes the two forms were mixed. Both forms were used for memorials, as at Jelling, but there are also runic charms and graffiti. Runic writing began to die out after the arrival of Christianity, as this led to the gradual introduction of the Roman alphabet.

▷ *The Rök stone in Ostergötland, Sweden, has the longest known runic inscription.*

Skalds and sagas

When Vikings gathered to enjoy a meal, men called *skalds* often entertained them by reciting poems, for example about Viking history or in honor of a listening leader. *Skalds* usually memorized these works, but sometimes wrote them down in runes. After the **Roman alphabet** arrived, most *skalds* put their poems in books instead.

The **saga**-writers also wrote in the Roman alphabet, and used both information and quotations from skaldic writings.

Fantasy or Fact?

According to Viking mythology, the god Odin discovered runes. In fact, people began to use these symbols, which are made up of straight lines, in pre-Viking times. Experts think the lack of curves was deliberate, because it makes runes easy to carve in wood, stone, or other hard material.

From the 1800s to the present, **archaeologists** have made major finds all over the Viking world. Their work has allowed historians to create a more accurate picture of this world and its people than was possible before, when they could rely only on **sagas** and guesswork.

Over the past two centuries, archaeology has changed in many ways. In the early days, it was often a pastime for rich men, who wanted above all to find glittering treasures—fast. Gradually, it has become a serious field of study in which science plays an important part, and evidence is slowly and carefully gathered. Increasingly, too, archaeologists are as interested in the lives and possessions of ordinary workers as of kings, queens, and **nobles**. These general changes in archaeology have had particular effects at Viking sites. At Birka, Hjalmar Stolpe pioneered the use of careful excavation. At L'Anse-aux-Meadows, radiocarbon dating combined with excavation was used to prove that Vikings reached North America. And at places as different as Repton and Gotland, experts have tried to find out what everyday life was like for ordinary people. Today, excavations are continuing all over the Viking world.

Lake Tissø

At Lake Tissø in Denmark, archaeologists are **excavating** a huge manor house. Interest in the area began in 1977, when a beautiful gold necklace was unearthed there. A team from the Danish National Museum, led by Lars Jørgensen, finally started the first of many digs at the site in 1995. More than

△ *These finely made silver and bronze jewelry pieces are among the many treasures found at Tissø.*

10,000 objects have been found, including exquisite items of jewelry. Their high quality suggests that the manor house was once used by kings, but probably only as a temporary residence for feasts and celebrations. The discovery of many miniature sculptures of the god Thor's hammer indicates that the manor was also a center for religious rituals.

The Fröjel Discovery Program

Fröjel is a harbor in Gotland where excavations began in 1998. Archaeologists are trying to find out more about the layout of the harbor and neighboring settlement, and about the area's trade links with other parts of the world. By excavating the local church and graveyards, they also hope to learn when and how Christianity was introduced in the area.

▽ *Visitors to Fröjel, Gotland, take part in the archaeological project to excavate graves.*

The excavations are part of the Fröjel Discovery Program, which aims to involve ordinary people in archaeological projects. Some digs are open to the general public and to schoolchildren, and foreign students are encouraged to visit as well. When the excavations are over, the site will become a visitor center, both to provide jobs and to let people enjoy the benefits of archaeologists' hard work for years to come.

DID YOU KNOW? The gold necklace found at Lake Tissø weighed 4 pounds (1.8 kilograms)!

793

In the first known Viking **raid**, Norwegians attack a **monastery** on Lindisfarne in northeast England.

9th century

An elaborate ship burial of two women takes place in Oseberg, Norway.

About 800

The Viking trading colony of Birka is founded on the Swedish island of Björkö.

829–831

Ansgar, a German monk, journeys to Denmark and to Birka in Sweden to try to **convert** people to Christianity.

850s

Ansgar makes further **missionary** visits to Scandinavia.

The Viking ship found at Gokstad by 19th-century **archaeologists** is built.

866

The Viking Great Army arrives in England from Denmark.

About 870–930

Vikings from Norway and elsewhere establish a settlement in Iceland.

About 873–874

The Danish Great Army camps at Repton in Derbyshire, England. Many soldiers and others die in an epidemic.

878

Alfred the Great defeats the Viking Great Army at the Battle of Edington. England is then divided between the western part, under Alfred's rule, and the northeastern part, controlled by the Vikings (the *Danelaw*).

911

Charles the Simple, king of France, grants Norwegian Vikings an area of northern France. It becomes known as Normandy.

930–1271

The *Althing* (national **assembly**) meets every summer in Thingvellir, Iceland.

About 958

Danish King Gorm is buried at Jelling.

958–987

King Harald Bluetooth, Gorm's son, rules Denmark and in about 960 begins to introduce Christianity there.

About 960 and about 980

Erik the Red is forced to leave first Norway, and then Iceland, as a punishment for murder.

About 985

Erik the Red settles in Greenland and establishes a Viking community there.

About 985–986

Bjarni Herjolfsson probably becomes the first Viking to see the coast of North America when blown off course on a voyage to Greenland.

1000

Leif Eriksson, son of Erik the Red, founds a short-lived Viking colony in North America and calls it Vinland.

Icelandic Vikings adopt Christianity.

About 1005

Icelandic Viking Thorfinn Karlsefni creates a more permanent settlement in North America after the departure of Leif Eriksson. But the hostility of the Native Americans and the difficulty of obtaining supplies from Iceland cause the settlers to leave after three years.

1014

Olaf Haraldsson becomes King of Norway and begins to convert the country to Christianity.

1066

The descendants of Norwegian Vikings who settled in Normandy, France, in 911, invade England. After defeating King Harold II, William the Conqueror, their leader, becomes England's ruler.

1067–1148

Life of Icelandic historian Ari the Learned.

11th century

Denmark and Norway become united Christian countries ruled by strong kings and the Viking Age ends there.

12th century

Sweden becomes the last Viking country to develop a stable, Christian monarchy and the whole Viking Age draws to a close.

13th century

Life of Icelandic historian and **saga** writer Snorri Sturluson.

The *Poetic Edda* and the *Prose Edda* are compiled in Iceland.

TIMELINE OF VIKING ARCHAEOLOGY

1820

Archaeologists **excavate** the North Mound in Jelling, Denmark, hoping to find the remains of Thyri, a 10th-century queen. They find only animal bones and **grave goods**.

1860s

Archaeologists at Jelling's South Mound look for the remains of King Gorm, Thyri's husband, but find nothing.

1871

Swedish archaeologist Hjalmar Stolpe begins excavations in the Viking trading colony of Birka, Sweden. He discovers 1,100 graves and impressive grave goods from around the world.

1880

Archaeologists, led by Nicolay Nicolaysen, President of the Antiquarian Society in Oslo, Norway, excavate a burial mound in Gokstad. The Viking ships they uncover include one in which a king was buried.

1904

Gabriel Gustafsson, a Swedish professor and director of the University Museum in the Norwegian city of Oslo, leads the team that excavates the ship burial in Oseberg, Norway.

1932

Archaeologists from the National Museum of Denmark carry out the first excavations at Brattahlid, Greenland, where Norwegian Viking Erik the Red established a farming settlement in the 900s.

1940s

Further excavations at Jelling's North Mound produce no significant finds.

1956

Divers discover the remains of a Viking sailing ship in Roskilde **Fjord**, Denmark. Danish archaeologist Dr. Ole Crumlin-Pedersen begins excavations, finding five different Viking ships.

Mid-1960s

Dr. Knud Krogh from the National Museum of Denmark leads new excavations at Jelling and discovers a grave under the church. The human bones it contained are probably those of King Gorm.

1960s–1970s

Dr. Knud Krogh leads more excavations at Brattahlid in Greenland.

1960s–1990s

Dr. Björn Ambrosiani from Sweden's Museum of National Antiquities leads excavations in the Viking trading colony of Birka.

1961–68

Archaeologist Anne Stine Ingstad and explorer Helge Ingstad, her husband, excavate the remains of a Viking settlement in L'Anse-aux-Meadows, Newfoundland. They attempt to show that it is the site of Leif Eriksson's Vinland.

1965

Yale University publishes the "Vinland Map," which is said to prove that the Vikings visited North America.

1970s

A team of Swedish archaeologists continue work in L'Anse-aux-Meadows. They agree that it is a Viking settlement.

The "Vinland Map" is shown to be a fake.

1974–88

Archaeologists Berthe and Martin Biddle discover and excavate a Viking **enclosure** in Repton, England. It proves to be the site of a winter camp used by the Danish Great Army.

1977

A Viking necklace made of gold and weighing 4 lb (1.8 kg) is unearthed at Lake Tissø in Denmark.

1986

Archaeologists working at Repton discover a mass grave outside the Viking enclosure. The remains inside probably belong to people who died of disease rather than in battle.

1995

Lars Jørgensen, an archaeologist from the Danish National Museum, begins excavations on the site of a Viking manor house at Lake Tissø in Denmark. So far, about 10,000 Viking objects have been discovered there.

1998

Archaeologists begin to excavate the Viking harbor of Fröjel on the Swedish island of Gotland. In the 21st century, they are still working there as part of the Fröjel Discovery Program.

1999

Two huge coin **hoards** from the Viking era are found on Gotland.

2002–2006

Experts from Iceland's Institute of Archaeology plan excavations at the *Althing* site of Thingvellir.

amber

clear, orange-brown, hardened sap that oozed out of ancient trees. Pieces of amber are often used to make jewelry.

Anglo-Saxon

of or relating to the people who were the main inhabitants of England when the Vikings arrived. They were descendants of the Angles, Saxons, and other tribes who had moved to England from Germany.

archaeologist

person who studies the past by examining and scientifically analyzing old objects and ruins

artifact

object made by people, such as a tool or an ornament. Archaeologists often use the word "artifacts" to describe the objects they find that were made by people in past times.

assembly

group of people formally gathered for a particular purpose, for example to discuss politics or make laws

bishop

senior Christian priest who governs one of the dioceses (districts) into which the Christian Church is divided

breeches

leg coverings that extend from the waist to the knee. Vikings often wound strips of cloth around the lower part of their legs, from knee to ankle, to keep them warm and dry.

campaign

series of battles and other activities designed to achieve a long-term military aim, for example conquering a particular country

cell

tiny piece of matter from which every part of the human body is made. DNA is contained in the central area of each cell, called the nucleus.

convert

change, or cause someone to change, religious beliefs

crosier

stick with a cross or hook at the top, similar to the sticks once carried by shepherds. Bishops carry crosiers as a sign of their duty to look after Christians as shepherds care for sheep.

driftwood

piece of wood washed up on the seashore or the edge of a lake

enclosure

area of land, water, or both, surrounded by a ditch, wall, or other barrier

excavate

dig up a building or area of land in order to look for ancient objects, ruins, or other evidence of the past

fertility

ability to have children; ability to produce good crops

fjord

narrow area of water that extends inland from the coast and has high cliffs on either side

forge

workplace of a blacksmith. There, metal is heated to make it soft, then beaten into new shapes, for example to make tools and weapons.

freeman

man who belonged to the class of Vikings between royalty and nobility at the top, and slaves at the bottom

grave good

object buried with a body in a grave. Grave goods are often precious items that a person owned when alive and wanted to keep with them after death.

hearth

fireplace, especially one that is on the floor in the middle of a room

hoard

hidden stock of treasure

hull

main body of a ship, part is above water and part is below water when the ship is sailing

ivory

hard, cream-colored material from which walrus and elephant tusks are made

jetty

small pier that sticks out into the sea or other area of water

kiln

type of oven in which newly made pottery is dried and hardened

knorr

wide, deep type of Viking ship used for carrying cargo. *Knorrs* had both a sail and oars.

longship

narrow, shallow type of Viking ship with a high, curved stem (front) and stern (back). Viking warriors went on raids in longships, which had both a sail and oars.

loom
large, often upright frame on which strands of wool, linen, or other fiber are woven into cloth

loot
stolen goods

missionary
person who sets out to change people's religious beliefs, especially by converting them to Christianity

monastery
building where a community of monks, and sometimes also nuns, lives, works, and worships

myth
tale about gods or other superhuman creatures. Ancient myths often set out to explain how the world began, why dramatic natural events (such as earthquakes) happen, and why people behave the way they do.

navigation
skill of finding routes from place to place and of guiding ships safely along these routes

noble
man belonging to the high class of Vikings

paganism
system of religious belief that, unlike Judaism, Christianity, and Islam, involves the worship of many gods

parliament
group of people that meets regularly to discuss political matters and make laws

radioactive
substance giving off energy in the form of particles or waves. By measuring the number of particles or waves given off, scientists can often work out how old the substance is.

raid
attack and steal from; violent attack during which goods are usually stolen

Roman alphabet
alphabet that the Romans developed to write Latin, and that is now used to write English and many other European languages

ruin
building or group of buildings that has fallen down or been destroyed

rune
one of the symbols that Vikings used to write on hard surfaces, such as stone

sacrifice
kill an animal or person and offer it to a god as part of a religious ritual; killing of a person or animal in this way

saga
any of the books written in medieval Iceland and Scandinavia that tell both mythical stories about gods and factual stories about historical events. Many of the stories are set in Viking times.

sledge
simple, open vehicle that is designed to travel over snow and is drawn by animals such as reindeer. The main part sits on top of two narrow wooden strips called runners.

spindle
stick with a slot in the top designed to prepare wool for weaving

tapestry
fabric made by weaving strands of colored thread together, and often featuring a picture or pattern

turf
grass dug up from the ground with roots and soil attached

FURTHER READING

Chapman, Gillian. *The Vikings.* Chicago: Heinemann Library, 2000.

Devereux, Paul. *Archaeology: The Study of Our Past.* Milwaukee: Gareth Stevens, 2002.

Orna-Ornstein, John. *Archaeology: Discovering the Past.* New York: Oxford University Press, 2002.

Rees, Rosemary. *The Vikings.* Chicago: Heinemann Library, 2002.